D0934914

My Editor

M. B. Goffstein

MY EDITOR

Farrar, Straus & Giroux
New York

This man
reads my work,
gnawing a cuticle.
Great! It's torn,
neat and clean.
He deserves this
quick success
in his work.

As he reads
my new book
in his cubicle,
I sit across
from his desk,
torn with love
I can't express,

because I'm not
the same person
who wrote
what he reads
with such great
yet divided attention.

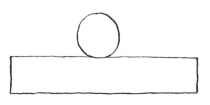

At home alone,

sitting

on the couch

in my room,

staring into space,

I think

and erase,

think and erase.

This painful process
would rip a sheet
of paper,
but my mind
is thicker.

When I strike
something hard,
I keep calm,
saying it over,
cleaning it off.

I get up
to take a pen
and paper,
make each letter:
yes, those lines
of words
are sound.

I'm an archaeologist
who's found her
site.

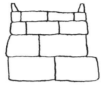

Day and night
I work hard
to rebuild
a little temple
no one knows
is there.

Lonesome

for my editor,

I call him

on the phone.

He used to say,

"Press on."

Now he says,

"Sounds good,"

or "Interesting,"

or "Hm."

Greatly encouraged
by this brush
with reality,
I begin to
hurry,
leaving some parts
buried,

and complete
my little structure
slightly
out of kilter.

I can't wait
until I shower,
dress,
chat with
a cab driver,
and deliver
my new book
to my editor!

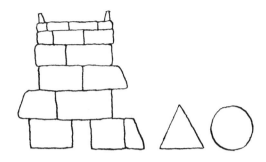

He sees at once
where it's
missing
some stones.

"Oh, it's not,"
I assure him.
I don't want
to return
to the country
of origin.
"Think about it,"
he tells me.

I am thinking:
No one sought
this little temple;
now it's found,
leave it alone.

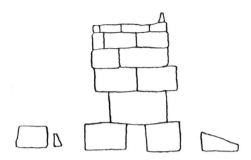

But he pokes here
and pushes there,
to see where
it caves in.

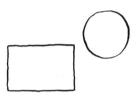

Sitting alone
at the desk
in my room,
I can't find
the buried words.
I try this,
I try that,
making lines up.

I try them
on my editor.
One, he says,
"locks into place."
I begin
to dig again,
and lose myself
in the excavation.

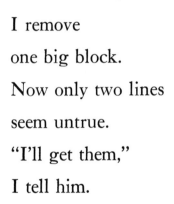

I remove
one big block.
Now only two lines
seem untrue.
"I'll get them,"
I tell him.

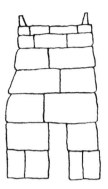

But my building
worries me.
It's stone-cold,
and I cry,
"Why not
have left it
wobbly?"

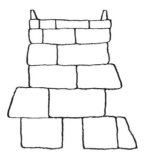

I tear it apart
and rebuild it
the old way.
Take it apart
and remake it
the new way.

Take it apart,
and suddenly see
how it goes.
"Why," my editor
comically wonders,
"did this take you
so long?"

Publication's
not the miracle,
but the friendship
of this man
for the me
I hardly know
but represent:

freshly showered,
in a plaid shirt,
trying to act
intelligent.